Facts
and
Figures

A Book of Tid-Bits & Trivia

By Dave Sommerhauser

◇ ◇ ◇

Illustrated By Art Heyne

Introduction

Well, here we go again. You are about to embark on
reading the sequel to "The F Book". I would like to
state that by reading this book you will not instantly
become the smartest cookie in the box. You will
however find some interesting facts, laugh a little,
disagree on some statements, and wonder why. Why
did they do that? Why did they do this? Why did this
fact make the book? Why can't I put this book down.
If you enjoy this book and would like to get a copy of
the first book in the series "The F Book" see the back
page. If you didn't like this book, let us know why.

ISBN: 0-7392-0071-2

Library of Congress Catalog Card Number: 98-91093

Printed in the USA by

MORRIS PUBLISHING
3212 East Highway 30 • Kearney, NE 68847 • 1-800-650-7888

Who coined the word "hello" and introduced it as the proper way to answer a telephone call ? Alexander Graham Bell favored "ahoy" but lost out to Thomas Edison, whose hello was derived from halloo, the traditional call to rouse hounds to the chase.

The actual playing time in a big league baseball game which last two and a half hours has been clocked at 9 minutes and 55 seconds.

When German automaker Gottlieb Daimler designed his new car he decided to name it after his daughter, Mercedes Daimler.

The average number of days that an American is in a bad mood each year, is 110. The percentage of Americans who are in a good mood every day, is 2%.

Every two thousand frowns creates one wrinkle.

So you won't have to go out on your lawn and count, I'll tell you. According to the Lawn Institute, there are approximately 564,537,600 blades of grass in an acre of lawn. They obviously have never seen my weed patch.

Maine is the only state in the U.S. that has one syllable.

The Olympic motto is "Citius Altius Fortius". The english translation of this motto is Faster, Higher, Stronger.

Did you know that Elton John legally changed his name to Elton John in 1971, from Reginald Kenneth Dwight. His full legal name is Elton Hercules John.

Do you know what Poponology is the study of? Beards.

When the paint was stripped from the White House for the first time in the 1980's, they had to remove 42 coats.

Chrysler built the B-29's that bombed Japan. Mitsubishi built Zeros that tried to shoot them down. Both companies now build cars in a joint plant called Diamond Star.

In 1913, the Electo-Alkaline Company of Oakland, California started selling bleach in jugs carried by horse drawn carts. A friend pointed out that their name sounded dangerous. He suggested that they combine the names of two of the products ingredients, "chlorine" and "sodium hydroxide" to create Clorox.

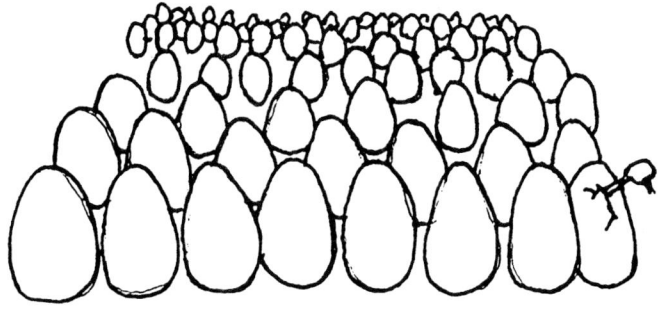

The average American eats 286 eggs per year

Surveys show that at a bar, lawyers and doctors are among the worst tippers. If you had to pick "the worst tipper" it would be doctors.

The fur on a Polar Bears is not white, it is clear. Their skin is actually black. Their hair is hollow and acts like fiber optics, directing sunlight to warm their skin. To help camouflage themselves more completely during a hunt they cover their black nose with their paws.

The first electric watches (battery operated) were patented in the 1950's.

You probably never gave it much thought, but the U.S. Department of Agriculture did. In a study using your tax dollars they concluded that for a meatball to be called a meatball, it must be made up of at least 65% meat.

Female canaries cannot sing.

According to the Chicago-based International Customer Service Association you are not the only one who has things that go wrong.

~ ~ ~ ~ ~

> 5,517,200 cases of soft drinks produced in the next 12 months will be flat.
> 2,488,200 books will be shipped with the wrong cover in the next 12 months.
> 2,000,000 documents will be lost by the IRS this year.
> 268,500 defective tires will be shipped this year.
> 114,500 mismatched pairs of shoes will be shipped this year.
> 22,000 checks will be deducted from the wrong bank account in the next 60 days.
> 18,322 pieces of mail will be mishandled in the next hour.
> 3,506 copies of tomorrows Wall Street Journal will be missing one section.
> 1,314 phone calls will be misplaced in the next minute.
> 12 babies will be given to the wrong parents each day.

The comic strip Peanuts was originally called Li'l Folks.

In costume jewelry, when gold is electroplated to metal, how thick must the layer of gold be? At least seven millionths of an inch thick, and the gold must be at least 10 karat.

The biggest room in the world, is the room for improvement.

The amount of tropical rain-forest cut down each year is the size of Tennessee.

What is Dorothy's last name in the movie The Wizard of Oz ? Next time you watch it, look on the mail box. You'll see the name, Gale.

Smokey the Bear's original name was Hot Foot Teddy.

What magazine did the Library of Congress cease to publish in Braille in 1985 after Congress voted to withhold funding? Believe it or not it was Playboy, which it had been publishing in Braille (without ads or pictures) for 15 years. Publication resumed in 1986 after the courts ruled that the action of Congress was illegal.

A cow will belch about 2 times a minute. I hope you weren't eating when you read this one.

An average person spends over 6 months of their lives waiting for the light to turn green.

There are 293 ways to make change for a dollar. Maybe that's why some clerks are so slow.

The World Trade Center, which stands on only 2 acres can accommodate 130,000 people.

Did you know that the Japanese scientists have invented square watermelons. Why, you ask ? So they will stack better.

Have you ever went to McDonalds and had a "McSpaghetti" or a "McLak"? Well, you can order them in the Philippines and in Norway, respectively.

I have a sure fire way for you to double your money. Fold it in half and put it in your pocket.

Space Facts:

~ More than 1 million planets the size of earth will fit inside of the sun.

~ The sun burns 9 million gallons of gas a second.

~ Because of the force of gravity, a person who weighs 150 pounds on earth would weigh 2 tons on the sun.

~The moon is only about one quarter the size of the earth.

The first Volkswagen Beetle hit the U.S. in 1949.

What King became president of the United States? Leslie King. When his parents divorced he was adopted by his stepfather and given a new name, Gerald Ford.

When Shell oil first opened its doors for business, it was a seashell novelty shop.

Of all the things you wear, your expression is the most important.

On the new one hundred dollar bill, the time on the clock tower of Independence Hall is 4:10.

Native Americans spoke more than 133 different languages.

The movie "Waynes World" was filmed in 2 weeks.

I'll bet this is something you really wanted to know. The Phillips screwdriver was invented in Oregon.

The Chameleon is not the only animal that can change colors. The Arctic fox is red and brown. However, in the middle of winter it changes color to pure white.

The largest gold nugget ever found was the Holtermann nugget. The nugget weighed 7,560 ounces. That is a little over 472 pounds.

We all know that an Octopus has 8 arms. Did you know that it has 3 hearts?

Some years ago a man who was over sixty was offered nearly $200,000 for a restaurant,motel, service station business that he had spent his life building. He loved the business and turned the offer down because he wasn't ready to retire. Two years later at the age of 65, he was flat broke with no income but a small social security check each month. The state had built a new highway, by passing his business and he lost everything. Most people would have been crushed but he refused to give up. There was one thing he knew how to do and that was how to fry chicken. Maybe he could sell his knowledge to others. He kissed his wife good bye and in a battered old car with a pressure cooker and a can of specially prepared flour, he set out to sell the idea to other restaurants. It was tough going and many nights he had to sleep in the car. But a few years later, he had built a nationwide franchised restaurant chain called Kentucky Fried Chicken. The man was Colonel Sanders.

Do you know what the difference is between skill and intelligence? Skill is successfully walking a tightrope stretched between the twin towers of the World Trade Center in New York. Intelligence, is not trying.   ~ 11 ~

How much ground can an average snail cover in an hour? About 25 feet.

To acquire knowledge one must study.
To acquire wisdom one must observe.

Marge Schott, owner of the Cincinnati Reds told her staff in 1995 she couldn't afford Christmas bonuses and gave candy instead. The candy turned out to be free samples from a baseball card company with coupons inside inviting customers to "win a free trip to the 1991 Grammys." In other words the candy was 4 years old.

Cars first came out with seat belts in 1950.

Young American women drink an average of one and a half cans of regular cola every day. That is the equivalent of 15 teaspoons of sugar.

Did you know that a male lightning bug has a distinctively different flash then of the female lightning bug. It is generally accepted that this is how they attract each other.

The first color television broadcast was sent over the air by CBS in 1951.

Baseball's first perfect game was pitched by "Cy" Young in 1904.

Have you ever wondered why Cheerios don't sink? The Cheerio dough is forced through a die that turns it into a long pasta-like tube. That tube is then sliced and thrown into a pressure chamber that puffs up the pieces. The air gives them their buoyancy.

Ancient Egyptians shaved off their eyebrows to mourn the death of their cats.

There are more beetles than any other type of creature in the world.

The face of a penny can hold about 30 drops of water.

An elephant can lift over a ton with it's trunk. However, if you visit a circus you will see the elephant standing quietly, held to a little post by only a thin piece of rope or chain. Why doesn't the elephant break free? Well, while still young and weak, the elephant is tied by a super heavy chain to an immovable stake. No matter how much the elephant tries and pulls he cannot break free. Soon he stops trying and accepts his limited fate. No matter how big and strong the elephant grows, he continues to believe that he cannot move as long as he sees that he is tied to a stake in the ground.

The worlds first beer can was produced on January 24th. 1935, in Richmond Virginia.

The United States Government does not allow portraits of living people to appear on postage stamps.

Cary Grant was nicknamed "El Squeako" by his friends. He counted the number of firewood logs in his mansions' garage and he used a marking pen to mark to level of the milk in the milk bottles in the refrigerator. This way he knew if his servants had used any milk.

A shrimps heart is in its head.

What does Baskin Robbins Ice Cream, Hallmark Cards, Apple Computers, Nike Shoes, and Walt Disney Productions all have in common? They all started out as a home based business.

Why does a slight tax increase cost you hundreds of dollars and a substantial tax cut save you sixty cents.

Did you know ???

- That in 1960, 15% of managers were women. In 1993, 43 % were.

- In 1990, 4.5% of the directors of Fortune 500 companies were women.

- One in four working mothers is a single parent. One in 25 working fathers is a single parent.

- In 1950, women made up 29.6% of the civilian labor force. In 1994, they made up 46.4%.

The can opener was invented 48 years after the can was invented.

If you were the only person in the world who could see, would you paint your house?

Diet Pepsi was originally called "Patio Diet Cola."

Actor Warren Beatty and Shirley MacLaine are brother and sister.

Intelligence is not what you know; it's what you understand.

The name Eggo, as in Eggo Waffles, has been around longer than you think. It was first used in 1935, when three brothers Frank, Tony, and Sam Dorsa borrowed $35.00 to buy a waffle iron and start experimenting with waffle batter. After they got the batter they liked, they started selling it to restaurants in northern California. A fourth brother George suggested that they call their product "Eggo" because of all the eggs in the batter. After World War II, when Americans started buying home freezers, the Dorsas thought that there was a bigger market for frozen waffles than for waffle batter. In 1950 they gambled and switched the entire production to ready made waffles. Within a year they were putting out 10,000 waffles an hour, and still couldn't keep up with the demands. Kellogg's bought the company in 1968 and today Eggo sales are over 300 million each year.

If you could keep a standard size pencil sharp, you could draw a light line for 35 miles, before the lead ran out.

A woodpecker can peck at a rate of 20 times per second. I'll bet you will sleep better tonight, now that you know that.

Air cushioned sneakers do not have any air in them. At first Nike tried air and it didn't work, it leaked through the "air-bag" material. They replaced the air with a gas that has larger molecules than air.

You knew that the first thing investigators look for in a plane crash is the "black box." Did you know that the box is actually yellow?

Over 50 million hot dogs are eaten In the United States every day.

Actor John Wayne made more than 200 movies.

What year was this?
The Dodge Dart Swinger was $2,100.
A Chevy Camaro was $2,454.
Bacon was 88 cents a pound.
Ham was 39 cents a pound.
Eggs were 19 cents a dozen.
Eye glasses and frames were $12.50
A 6 pack of Busch beer was 98 cents.
 * (The answer is at the bottom of this page)

Do you know the difference between an error and a mistake? An error becomes a mistake when you refuse to admit it.

The glue on Israeli stamps is certified kosher.
* (Answer ... 1970)

A cat needs 1/6 the amount of light that a human needs to be able to see.

The first wooden golf tee was patented in 1899, by a Boston dentist, Dr. George F. Grant. Until then the ball was placed on a small pile of sand to enable the golfer to tee off.

More than 50% of Americans fall asleep on their side.

It takes 6 months to build a Rolls Royce .... and 13 hours to build a Toyota.

The oldest brewery founded in the United States is the Yuengling Brewery in Pottsville, Pennsylvania. It was founded in 1829.

Women blink nearly twice as much as men.

The Whistling swan has 25,216 feathers. That is more feathers than any other bird.

Six geese laying on the ground, like in the Christmas song, "On the First day of Christmas" is called a gaggle, but six geese flying in the air is a skein.

Statistics show that a published book will contain between ten and twenty spelling or grammatical errors. I'm sure that this book is no exception. Or then again, we might set a new standard.

A cat can run up to 31 miles per hour.

The first slot machine ever built is now in the Liberty Bell Restaurant & Casino in Reno Nevada.

You should not eat a crawfish with a straight tail. It was dead before it was cooked.

Peter Benchley, a first time author struggled for months to come up with a title for his book about a man eating shark. He tried hundreds of titles from "The Shark", to the "Great White", to A "Silence in the Water". Finally his editor said that there was only one word he liked in any of the titles, Jaws. By then Benchley didn't even care anymore: "Nobody reads first novels anyway".

Do you know who was the first Marvel Comics super hero? ---- The Human Torch.

A bowling pin only has to tilt 7.5 degrees in order to fall down.

Friendship is like a bank account. You can't continue to draw on it without making deposits.

Thomas Edison had 1,093 patents. Dr. Yoshiro Nakamats, inventor of the floppy disk, has 2,360 patents and still going.

Former basketball great Wilt Chamberlain was 7 ft. 1in. tall. His parents were both 5 ft. 8 in..

Boston's Telephone Dispatch Company issued the first personal phone directory in 1878, just two years after Alexander Graham Bell invented the telephone. It was different from todays White Pages in two ways.
1. It was only one page long, because only 97 Bostonians owned telephones in 1878.
2. It didn't list any phone numbers. Why not? There weren't any. Direct dialing hadn't been invented yet. You just picked up the receiver, turned the crank that rang a bell alerting the operator. When she came on the line, you told her the name of the person you wanted to talk to.

What is the only essential vitamin not found in the white potato? If you said vitamin A, you are correct.

Aristotle believed that the main purpose of the human brain was to cool the blood.

Illinois has the largest number of personalized license plates of any state.

Only one person was ever elected to both the baseball and the football Hall of Fame. If you think it was Carl Hubble, you are right.

The cost to construct a golf course today is in the millions of dollars. The cost to construct the original 6 hole golf course at The Country Club in Brookline, Massachusetts, in 1892 was $50.

King Kong was the only movie to have a sequel (*Son of Kong*) released in the same year (1933).

A road map will tell you everything you want to know except how to fold it up again.

The Nestles family has not run Nestles company since 1875.

Most of us will never do great things but we can do small things in a great way.

Tid bits on tigers.

> The Sumatran tiger has the most stripes of all tiger subspecies.
> The Siberian tiger has the fewest stripes.
> A tigers paw prints are called pug marks.

Most people take an average of seven minutes to fall asleep. It takes me seven minutes just to get the covers arranged properly.

Graham Crackers were invented around 1840 by Sylvester Graham not as a snack but as a source of dietary fiber to improve digestion.

The bubbles in Guiness beer sink to the bottom rather than float to the top like all other beers. No one knows why.

Did you know that it has been over 20 years since the Concord made its' first commercial flight? Time sure flies.

The Amazon rain-forest produces half of the world's oxygen supply.

Hersheys' Kisses are called that because the machine that makes them looks like it's kissing the conveyor belt.

The Red Sea was originally called the Reed Sea.

The main library at Indiana University sinks over an inch every year because when it was built, the engineers failed to take into account the weight of all the books that would occupy the building.

Kodak is the world's largest user of silver.

Back in 1912, a chocolate maker named Clarence Crane had a problem. He made only chocolate candy and during the summer months he had hardly any orders because the chocolate didn't ship well because of the heat. To help stay in business, Crane decided to produce hard candy mints during this time. Crane's factory wasn't set up for making hard candy, so he hired a pill manufacturer for the job. Most mints of that time were square and pillow-shaped, plus expensive to produce. Crane ordered his new mints to be flat and round, with a hole in the middle, to be different. "They look like little lifesavers," Crane said. Suddenly the mints had a name. Still, for Crane the mints were only a sideline. When a New York ad salesman Edward John Noble tried to persuade him to advertise the mints, Crane wasn't interested. "You'll make a fortune!" Noble said. "Think so?" Crane replied. "You buy the brand." So for $2,900 Noble bought the rights and went to work. He talked drugstores and restaurants into the idea of putting them near the cash register with a big 5 cent card. "Be sure every customer gets a nickel back with their change," he told them. His marketing idea worked, and Life Savers' familiar little roll became one of the world's bestselling candies.

Hillbillies medical terminology for the layman.

◇ ◇ ◇ ◇

Artery ------------ The study of fine paintings.
Barium ----------- What you do when CPR fails.
Coma ------------ A punctuation mark.
Dilate ------------ To live longer.
Fester ----------- Quicker.
Hangnail -------- A coathook.
Minor Operation-Coal digging.
Morbid ---------- A higher offer.
Nitrate ----------- Lower than day rate.
Outpatient ------ A person who has fainted.
Protein ---------- In favor of young people.
Tablet ----------- A small table.
Tumor ---------- An extra pair.
Post Operative - A letter carrier.
Urine ------------ Opposite of your out.
Congenital ----- Friendly.
Serology ------- A study of English Knighthood.
Varicose Veins- Veins that are very close.
Benign --------- What you are after you are
                       eight.

Chia Pets, you know the little animal looking things that you water and grow grass on, are only sold in December.

In the late 1800's, a manufacturer approached Sam Loyd, one of America's premier game designers, with a problem. His company had a surplus of cardboard squares. Could Loyd devise some sort of game that would use the squares, so his company could get rid of them? Borrowing from a century old Indian game called *pachisi,* Loyd created a "new" game called Parcheesi. It didn't take him very long. In fact, it was so easy that he only charged the manufacturer $10.00 for his services. Within a few years, the game became one of the most popular games in the United States, but that $10.00 was the only money Loyd ever received for creating it.

Boston was the first U.S city with a subway.

A full grown bear can run as fast as a horse for a short distance.

In order for a deck of cards to be mixed enough to play with properly, it should be shuffled at least 7 times.

Early in the Great Depression prepared mayonnaise went from a household staple to an expensive luxury item that few people could afford. Kraft began researching ways to make an inexpensive substitute and eventually came up with something made of oil, egg yolks, cooked starch paste, and seasonings. It had less oil than regular mayonnaise, so it was cheaper to produce, but it was also harder to make. To help with this problem Kraft invented a new mixer they called the "miracle whip" which gave the product its creamy consistency. Then they named the product after the machine.

Remember the Frisbee? It was the latest fad in 1957. If you had invented it you would be reading this book on your yacht.

Johnny Miller was the first golf pro to be elected into the Golf Hall of Fame by a ballot vote. To achieve this, a player is required to receive 75% of the vote.

In the United States we have various coins. We have the 1 cent, 5 cent, 10 cent, 25 cent, 50 cent, and $1.00 coins. Did you know that at one time the United States had the half cent piece, as well as the 2 cent, 3 cent and 20 cent piece.

The electric chair was adopted by New York for capitol punishment in 1889.

If your ever walking along with someone and they tell you they see Crotalus Atrox, you have a reason to be afraid. They're trying to tell you they see a Western Diamond-Back Rattlesnake.

The 1913 Liberty head 5 cent piece was the first coin to be sold for more than a million dollars.

The raised reflective dots in the middle of highways are called Botts dots. Another simple thing you should have invented.

Johnny Carson gave 4,531 monologues during his 30 years as host of the Tonite Show.

The word "girl" appears only once in the Bible.

All gondolas in Venice, Italy must be painted black, unless they belong to a high official.

Don't ever walk a cow upstairs because you will have to carry him back down the stairs. Although a cow can walk upstairs, his knees cannot bend properly to allow him to walk back down the steps.

Felix the Cat is the first cartoon character to have been made into a balloon for a parade.

When you see the French word *"brut"* on a wine bottle it means dry.

The first run of the Pony Express left St. Joseph, Missouri on April 3, 1860 and arrived in Sacramento, California ten days later. The Pony Express ended in October, 1861.

Winchester House in San Jose, California, was built by the creator of the winchester rifle. The house has 52 skylights, 47 fireplaces, 10,000 windows, 40 staircases, 2,000 doorways, and 13 bathrooms.

What is a California Long White? A white shark, no. A large surfing wave with a white crest, no. Nothing as exciting as that. It's a long white potato.

There are 132 rooms in theWhite House.

Tropical bats are the key elements in the rain forest ecosystems. The bats pollinate flowers and disperse seeds for trees and shrubs.

There are some unusual catfish in the world. There is one that can use its' fins to walk across mud. There's another that like the electric eel, discharges electric shocks to its enemies. Then, there is a meat eating catfish native to South America rivers. The most unique catfish species is known as Silvrus glanis. It is found in Europe and is a true giant. This catfish develops into a fifteen-foot, 660 pound whopper.

The only continent without reptiles or snakes is Antarctica.

Howdy Doody had forty-eight freckles. Now there's something you really needed to know.

The word "karate" means "empty hand."

Just in case rats come up in your conversation today, here are some facts for you to use:

~ Rats can go without water longer than camels.

~ Rats can fall from 50 feet and not get injured.

~ A pair of mated rats can produce up to 15,000 rat babies in just one year.

More Hollywood films have been made about boxing than about anything else.

It took Four people to play Darth Vader in Star Wars. David Prowse was his body, James Earl Jones did the voice, Sebastian Shaw was his face and a fourth person did the breathing.

Rhinos are in the same family as horses and are thought to have inspired the myth of the unicorn.

The first Bowie knife was forged in Washington, Arkansas.   ~ 35 ~

Stewardesses and reverberated are the two longest words you can type using only the left hand keys of your typewritter. The longest word that can be typed using only the right hand is lollipop.

Chop suey did not originate in China. It was first made in New York City by a Chinese cook trying to whip something together for his employers guests. When they ask him what the dish was call he said "Chop suey" translated in English is "miscellaneous pieces or bits."

Heineken Beer originated in the early 1860's. A young Dutchman named Gerard Adriaan Heineken wanted to start his own business but he didn't have any money. His mother on the other hand did, and she hated the way drunks wandered the streets of Amsterdam on Sunday morning after a all-night Saturday binge. He suggested to his mother that if she help him start a brewery, local men might drink beer all night instead of hard liquor and public drunkenness might decrease. It was a pretty strange sales pitch, but it worked. Today Heineken is the largest beer producer in Europe and second largest in the world.

You could fit the 21 smallest states into Alaska.

In 1987 American Airlines saved $40,000 by eliminating one olive from the First Class salads.

The talking doll was not invented by Mattel or Tonka, it was invented in 1888, by Thomas Edison.

Camels have three eyelids to protect themselves from blowing sand.

Where is the world's largest K-Mart?
No matter what you answered I'd almost bet you where wrong. It is on the island of Guam.

Pecans are the only food that astronauts do not have to treat and dehydrate when flying in space.

Nine pennies weigh exactly one ounce.

There are two people in the baseball hall of fame that had nothing to do with baseball. They didn't coach, own a team, or play. I'll give you a clue. "Who's on first." --- That's right, Abbott and Costello.

Kermit the frog is left handed.

Texas is the only state that is allowed to fly their state flag at the same height as the United States flag.

The car in the foreground on the back of a $10 bill is a 1925 Huptmobile.

The quarts crystal in your wristwatch vibrates 32,768 times a second.

A king cobra is the biggest of all poisonous snakes growing over 13 feet long. When disturbed it raises its head and strikes its fangs straight through the victims skin. One bite from a king cobra can kill an elephant in four hours.

Drinking water after eating reduces the acid in your mouth by over 60 percent.

To be able to see a rainbow, your back must be to the sun.

Worcestershire Sauce is basically an anchovy ketchup.

The launching mechanism of a carrier ship that helps planes take off, could throw a pickup truck over a mile.

Americans will eat 90 acres of pizza today.

Fabrics and their origins:

Angora	Ankara, Turkey
Calico	Calicut, India
Cambric	Cambrai, France
Chambray	Cambrai, France
Damask	Damascus, Syria
Denim	Nimes, France
Gauze	Gaza, Palestine
Jersey	Jersey Island, U.K.
Lisle	Lille, France
Madras	Madras, India
Oxford Cloth	Oxford, U.K.
Tweed	Tweed River U.K.

The cheetah is the only cat in the world that can't retract its claws.

Abraham Lincoln once said "It's better to be silent and thought a fool than speak and remove all doubt."

There is a quarter pound of salt in every gallon of sea water.

A duck's quack doesn't echo, and no one knows why.

The placement of a donkeys eyes in its head allows it to see all four feet at the same time. Now you know why they are so sure-footed on mountain trails.

Americans use enough toilet paper in one day to wrap around the world 9 times. If it were on one giant roll, we would be unrolling it at the rate of 7,600 miles per hour - roughly mach. 10, or ten times the speed of sound. Sometimes I wonder where I get these facts and why. I must have had a weird childhood.

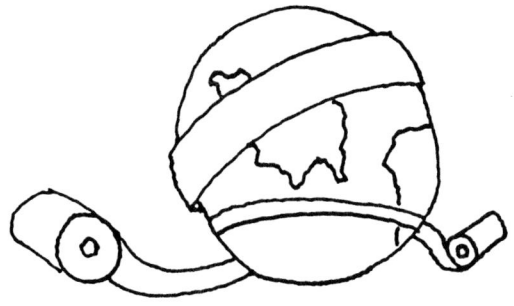

In the 1940's, the FCC assigned television's Channel 1 to mobile services (two way radios in taxi cabs, for instance) but did not renumber the other channel assignments. That is why your TV set has channel 2 and up.

A group of geese on the ground is a gaggle, a group of geese in the air is a skein.

Sony was originally called Tokyo Tsushin Kogyo. The founder, Akio Morita wanted a name he could market internationally. He looked through a Latin dictionary and picked out the word *sonus* (sound), and combined it with "sunny."

Ben and Jerry's Ice Cream Company gives its ice cream waste to Vermont farmers, who use it as pig feed. The pigs love it all....except for Mint Oreo, which they refuse to eat.

Hulk Hogan's real name is Terry Bollea.

Grey Poupon Dijon Mustard sounds like someone invented a pretty classy name. Actually, it is named for a British man named Mr. Grey and his French business partner Monsieur Poupon, who put up the money to open up the mustard factory in (where else?) Dijon, France.

Call it habit or call it superstition but Shirley Temple always had 56 curls in her hair.

The bull bird can make a *moo* sound like a cow.

Months that begin on a Sunday will always have a Friday the 13th.

The fingerprints of koala bears are virtually indistinguishable from those of humans. So much so that they could be easily confused at a crime scene.

The Dominican Republic has the only national flag with a bible pictured on it.

Zebras are born with brown and white stripes. As the animal grows older they turn to black and white. Also, no zebras are born with the same pattern of stripes.

If your wondering why the oak tree in your backyard doesn't have acorns, it's because the tree is not old enough. Oak trees do not have acorns until they are fifty years old or older.

Kangaroos cannot walk backwards.

Cats have over one hundred vocal sounds, while dogs have about ten.

Our eyes are the same size from birth, but our nose and ears never stop growing.

Cheerios cereal was originally called Cherry oats. In 1946, Quaker Oats threatened to sue, claiming it had exclusive rights to the name "Oats." Rather than fight, General Mills switched the name to Cheerios.

If you took a standard "Slinky" and stretched it out flat, it would measure 87 feet long.

Tennessee and Missouri are both bordered by eight states. That is more than any other state.

Poodles are the most popular registered dog in America.

After a coffee seed is planted, it takes five years to yield consumable fruit.

In every episode of Seinfeld there is a superman figure somewhere on the set.

After successfully inventing the game Twister, Reynolds Guyer decided to become a full time toy designer. He quit his job and started his own toy design company. One of his companies first ideas was a game based on cavemen. It involved hiding money under foam rocks and defending the money by throwing some of the foam rocks at your opponent. After a while they realized that the part of the game they really liked was throwing the foam rocks. Then someone decided that the rocks weren't as round as they liked, so they began trimming them with scissors into a better shape. Eventually they were almost round like balls. Guyer soon abandoned the caveman game and focused on the balls. He made up the name "Nerfs" to communicate what he thought of as their "soft, friendly nature." Within a decade Nerf became one of the largest lines of sports/action toys in the world.

Karl Benz invented the automobile in 1885.

The man who created the Thighmaster was once a Buddhist monk.

Coffee beans are not beans ---they're fruit pits.

The oldest pig in the world lived to the age of 68. I guess no one was hungry at the time.

Did you know that a cow can get "hardware disease" from eating nails, bolts, or other small metal objects that can be out in pastures and become seriously ill. To prevent this from happening, some farmers force their cows to swallow a three inch magnet. Because of the magnets size, it will remain in the cows stomach. When the cow eats another piece of metal, it will stick to the magnet, preventing it from moving on through the cow's digestive system where it can cause harm.

The first issue of Rolling Stone magazine appeared in 1967.

Barbie's full name is Barbara Millicent Roberts.

Personal computing took off in 1976 with the Apple I. The Apple II immediately followed , in 1977.

The year they started:

Charlie's Angels	1976
Soap	1977
Dallas	1978
Taxi	1978
20/20	1978
Magnum, P.I.	1980
Hill Street Blues	1981
Cheers	1982
The Cosby Show	1984
Miami Vice	1984

New Yorks Central Park is almost twice as big as the entire country of Monaco.

The Peregrine falcon can dive at a speed of up to 240 miles per hour. I have to ask myself "why?" At that speed what is he going to catch?

The Eiffel Tower (984 ft.) is more than three times taller than the Statue of Liberty (305 ft.).

Of the people who drink milk in the world, 55% of them drink goats milk.

You watch it every day but do you know what the word "television" means? It means "See at a distance".

Mattel toys got its name from the two founders, Harold Matson and Elliot Handler. Handler was in the picture frame business. In 1946 he had a lot of extra slats for framing, so he and Mr. Matson built doll furniture out of them.

There are more bagpipe bands in the U. S. than there are in Scotland.

Pregnant goldfish are known as "twits."

In the early 1920's, R. A. Watkins, the owner of a small printing plant in Illinois, was approached by a man who wanted to sell him the rights to a homemade device made of waxed cardboard and tissue. You could write on it, but the messages could be easily erased by lifting up the tissue. Watkins told the man that he would think about it and let him know. In the middle of the night, Watkins's phone rang; it was the man calling from jail. He told Watkins that if he would bail him out, he'd give Watkins the rights to the invention. Watkins agreed and got the rights which he then patented, and called "Magic Slate." Since then, tens of millions have been sold.

On a average day the various United States mints stamp out over 37 million pennies, 4.6 million nickels, 6.6 million dimes, 5.8 million quarters and 14,000 half dollars.

Now here's something you really needed to know. People who live in the city have longer, thicker, denser nose hair than people who live in the country.

When W. C. Fields traveled, he didn't like to carry a lot of cash so wherever he was, he opened a bank account. He claimed to have over 700 bank accounts all over the world. He usually opened these accounts under his real name but sometimes he used odd aliases like Figley E. Whitesides, Sneed Hearn, Dr. Otis Guelpe, and Senor Guillermo McKinley. After his death, only about three dozen accounts were located.

Encouraged by their mother to go into business together, Henry Bloch and his brother Richard formed the United Business Company in 1946. The plan was to provide bookkeeping, management, and other services to businesses, but they spent so much time helping their customers fill out tax forms that they decided to focus on tax preparation exclusively. To give their business a more personal touch, they decided to name the business after themselves. Rather than having customers mispronounce their name as "blotch," they change the spelling to match the way their name was pronounced. Today, H&R Block prepares one out of every ten tax returns filed with the Internal Revenue Service.

The silhouette on the NBA logo is Jerry West. The silhouette on the Major League Baseball logo is Harmon Killebrew.

The original idea for tombstones was that the weight pressing down on the body would not allow the ghost to float away. This must have been thought up by two guys in a bar, late at night.

The Pentagon, in Arlington, Virginia, has twice as many bathrooms as necessary. When it was built in the 1940s, the state of Virginia still had segregation laws requiring separate toilet facilities for blacks and whites.

I bet you never thought to look at the ingredients of A-1 Steak Sauce. It contains both orange peel and raisins.

The Lincoln head penny replaced the Indian head penny in 1909.

If your writing a poem, don't end a line with month. You will be in big trouble because no word in the English language rhymes with month.

If you have a great sense of smell and your in the middle of the woods and seem to smell fresh cut cucumbers, be careful. That is the smell of a poisonous copperhead snake.

In the Disney movie "Fantasia", the Sorcerer's name is "Yensid" (Disney spelled backwards).

Horses can't sit.

In 1970, a U.S. postage stamp cost eight cents.

Studebaker was the only major car company to stop manufacturing cars while making a profit on them.

In 1993, Barry Stroller, a Seattle drywall installer, took some Ex-Lax to cure his constipation. When it didn't work he wrote the company demanding his money back. The company mailed him a check but mistakenly entered his zip code as the amount. Stroller deposited the $98,002 in the bank, withdrew it a few days later...and hasn't been seen since.

If your a baseball fan and your old enough to remember Connie Mack, then you might be interested to know that his real name was Cornelius McGilicuddy.

Fingernails grow 1/25 of an inch each week.

The number of Alaskans that are licensed to fly is 1 out of 3.

The United States Capitol has 365 steps---one for each day of the year.

The federal government owns about 29% of the land in America.

How many times does the number 1 or the word one appear on a one dollar bill? ----------- 16

The cost of labor on a pair of Nike tennis shoes amounts to 4% of the retail cost. In other words, a pair of $75.00 tennis shoes cost $3.00 in labor to produce.

The beer can was created in 1935 in Richmond, Virginia.

If you are like most people and are asked how many islands make up the state of Hawaii you would say 6 or 7. Actually there are 132 islands that comprise the state of Hawaii. The number of inhabited islands is 7.

Some beer facts about Anheuser-Busch Beers.

^ Budweiser was created in 1876.

^ Michelob was created in 1896.

^ Anheuser-Busch is the worlds largest brewer.

^The A&Eagle logo was first used on the company's beer products in 1872 and symbolizes the company's century old heritage of pride and quality.

^ It takes up to 30 days or longer to brew an Anheuser-Busch product.

^ Budwieiser became the first beer to sponsor network television with the sponsorship of "The Ken Murray Variety Show" in 1951.

Fact: Travel agents worldwide awarded Antigua and Barbados the 1997 World Travel Award as the leading honeymoon destination in the world.

Pittsburgh is the only city where all major league sports have the same colors: Black and Gold.

A coat hanger is 44 inches long if straightened.

The King of Hearts is the only king in a deck of cards without a mustache.

Tina Turners real name is Annie Mae Bullock.

The football huddle originated at Gallaudet University in the 19th. century when the football team found out that the opposing team was reading their "hand signals" and interpreting plays. Gallaudet University is the worlds' only accredited four year liberal arts college for the deaf.

Captain Kirk never said "Beam me up Scotty." What he said was "Beam me up, Mr. Scott."

It is physically impossible for a pig to look straight up to the sky.

The little hole in the sink that lets the water drain out instead of flowing over the side is called a "porcelator."

Rita Hayworth's real name was Margarita Casino.

When the cruise liner Queen Elizabeth II was in service, it moved only six inches for each gallon of diesel fuel it burned.

A quarter has 119 grooves around the edge. A dime has 118 grooves.

The name of the dog on the Cracker Jack box is Bingo.

Gatorade was named for the University of Florida Gators where it was first developed.

A baby oyster is called a "spat."

On an American one dollar bill, there is an owl in the upper left-hand corner of the "1" encased in the "shield". There is also a spider hidden in the front upper right-hand corner.

New Jersey has a spoon museum featuring over 5,400 spoons from every state and almost every country.

Maine is the toothpick capitol of the world.

Sylvia Miles had the shortest performance that was ever nominated for an Oscar when she was in "Midnight Cowboy." Her entire role lasted only six minutes.

The tailless dinner jacket was invented in Tuxedo Park, New York. Thus it is called the "Tuxedo Dinner Jacket" and it is named after the town...not the other way around.

The giant squid has the largest eyes in the world.

Moisture, not air causes Super-Glue to dry.

Rhode Island is the smallest state yet it has the largest name. The official name used on all state documents is Rhode Island and Providence Plantations.

Cranberries are sorted for ripeness by bouncing them. A fully ripened cranberry can be dribbled like a basketball.

A full moon always rises at sunset.

Soldiers in every country salute with their right hand.

The numbers "172" can be found on the back of a five dollar bill in the bushes at the base of the Lincoln Memorial.

In 1963, baseball pitcher Gaylord Perry remarked, "They'll put a man on the moon before I hit a home run". On July 20, 1969 a few hours after Neil Armstrong set foot on the moon Gaylord Perry hit his first and only home run of his career.

In England, the Speaker of the House is not allowed to speak.

The "L. L." in L. L. Bean Catalog stands for Leon Leonwood.

A Chinese checkerboard has 121 holes.

Libya is the only country in the world with a solid, single-colored flag------it's green.

If you watched the very first "Gilligan's Island" you might know the skippers name. It was only mentioned once in the first episode on the radio newscast about the ship wreck. His name was Jonas Grumby.

Your stomach has to produce a new layer of mucus every two weeks otherwise it would digest itself.

Of the six men who made up the three stooges, three of them were real brothers, Moe, Curly and Shemp.

The highest point in Pennsylvania is lower than the lowest point in Colorado.

Most people think of Holland as the tulip capitol of the world. Actually the city of Mt. Vernon, Washington grows more tulips than the entire country of Holland.

Tigers have striped skin, not just striped fur.

The island of Guam does not have sand. The "sand" on the beaches is actually finely ground coral.

The only domestic animal not mentioned in the bible is the cat.

The home team must provide 36 footballs for each National League professional football game.

The correct response to the Irish greeting "top of the morning to you" is "and the rest of the day to yourself."

West Virginia and Maryland have no natural lakes.

Decator, Illinois was the original home of the Chicago Bears. Until they moved they where known as the Stalley Bears.

In 1969, the last Chevrolet Corvair to be made came off the assembly line. It was painted gold.

The longest recorded flight of a chicken is thirteen seconds.

If you have 3 quarters, 4 dimes and 4 pennies you would have $1.19. You also would have the largest amount of money in coins without being able to make change for a dollar.

Nutmeg is extremely poisonous if injected intra-venously.

What do these people all have in common? Hugh Beaumont, who played Ward Cleaver in "Leave it to Beaver, Mr. Rogers and Sir Isaac Newton? They were all ordained ministers.

The Los Angeles Rams were the first U. S. football team to introduce emblems on their helmets.

A good dart board is made out of horse hairs.

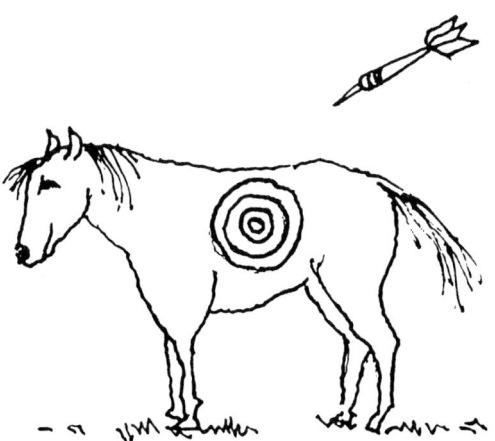

Only two people, John Hancock and Charles Thomson signed the Declaration of Independence on July 4th, 1776. Most of the others signed it on August 2nd. of that year.

Over 35 million pine trees are produced each year for Christmas.

Columbia University is the second largest land-owner in New York City, next to the Catholic Church.

Every major league baseball team buys about 18,000 baseballs a year.

The following are a list of some famous people who dropped their last name:

Eddie Albert   (Edward Albert Heimberger)
Ray Charles   (Ray Charles Robinson)
Joe Louis   (Joseph Louis Barrow)
Bela Lugosi   (Bela Lugosi Blasko)
Rudolph Valentino - Are you ready for this one?
(Rudolph Guglielmi di Valentina d'Antonguolla)

More men stutter than women.

Janet Guthrie is the only women to win the Indianapolis 500.

Hostess Twinkies are the creation of James A. Dewar, who ate a couple of them every day and lived to be eighty-eight. He is known to have said "Twinkies was about the best darn-tootin' idea I ever had." He came up with the idea when he noticed that bakers sold a lot of short-cake during strawberry season but couldn't give it away the rest of the year. He figured that if he stuffed some sort of cream filling in the short-cake, people would like it even without fruit. The first Twinkies were made in Chicago, in 1930 and were an immediate success. Although some people think that the shelf life of a Twinkie is 50 years, twinkies are discarded if they don't sell in four days.

If you pulled a starfishs' five arms off and threw them into the sea, a new starfish would generate from each arm.

Soccer is the world's most popular sport.

When a whale sleeps, half of its brain stays awake in case of approaching danger.

If you plan on growing your own Christmas tree I think you ought to know that it takes 6 to 10 years of fighting heavy rain, wind, drought and hail to get a mature 6 -7 foot Christmas tree.

The Pentagon spent $1,868 for each toilet seat on its C-5B cargo plane.

Colonel Sanders revealed his recipe for Kentucky Fried Chicken to just two living souls. One was his wife, Claudia and the other was Jack Massey, head of the three-man syndicate that purchased the Kentucky Fried Chicken Corporation from Sanders in 1964.

Footprints left on the moon by the Apollo astronauts will last about ten million years.

Sound travels about five times faster through water than through air.

Fred Norton of Clinton, Oklahoma is the only person to swim the Mississippi River lengthwise. He did it in 1931.

The shoe on your right foot will wear out faster than the shoe on your left foot.

Personal letters to the President of the United States have a secret numerical code. The President often gets 10,000 letters a day. All must be opened, read and answered by the White house mail staff. So that letters from friends get to the President and family unopened, all close friends are given a sequence of numbers to write on the outside of the envelope. The code changes with each President. Jimmy Carter, for example used an old phone number of his wife's.

In 1965 a company invented special motion film so viewers could smell things as they saw them. It was called "Smellavision" and if you're thinking that your nose isn't working at the movies, it's probably fine. Smellavision "stunk" so it never caught on.

Lemons are composed of more sugar than strawberries.

An ear of corn never has an odd number of corn rows.

The largest coney dog ever created was 102 feet long and weighed over 180 pounds.

Santa Claus is the most recognizable person to schoolchildren. Can you name the second most recognizable person to youngsters?
Ronald McDonald.

There is a little coding or gimmickry on U.S. mail. All U.S. postage stamps have an invisible ink coding that fluoresces in ultraviolet light. This is partially to deter counterfeiting of stamps but mostly it is to speed up the sorting. Canceling machines shine an ultraviolet beam on letters and check for a glow. Calcium silicate which glows orange-red and zinc orthosilicate which glows yellow-green are used. They are printed over the entire face of the stamp or in a geometric pattern.

In 1956 a women received a patent for inventing bird diapers. I'll go out on a limb and say that if she's rich today, it not from this invention.

Here's a tip for the next time you go in for an eye exam. Only nine letters are used on the standard Snellen eye chart. All occur at least once in the easy lines (1 through 5). So if you think you see a G down in the smaller print, it's a C or an O. There are no G's on the standard chart.

Sleeping burns more calories than watching TV.

William Moulton Marston is the man who invented the polygraph or lie detector. He also is the person who created the Wonder Woman comic strip under the name William Moulton.

Albert Einstein didn't speak until he was six years old. Who would have listened to his theories at four years old anyway.

You will grow about 1,000 new layers of skin in your lifetime.

The hamburger was 90 years old in 1994.

Coca Cola sells about half of all the soda in the world.

There are over 23,840 man-made objects orbiting the earth; over 15,417 belong to the United States.

Though Dr. Pepper is sometimes categorized as a cherry cola, the Dr. Pepper Company denies that it has either cherry or kola flavorings. Almost everything else that has been rumored to be in Dr. Pepper isn't in it. There isn't any black pepper, chile pepper, bell pepper, peppermint , or prune juice. The formula contains twenty-three ingredients and is locked in two separate bank vaults.

It takes a plastic six-pack ring about 450 years to decompose.

Do you have any idea what these things are?
Armsaye - Feat - Minimus - Peen - or Rasceta:

Armsaye is the armhole in clothing.

Feat is a dangling curl of hair.

Minimus is your little finger or toe.

Peen is the end of the hammer head opposite the striking face.

Rasceta are the creases on the inside of your wrist.

The Soviet Union has eleven time zones. That is more than any other country.

Nescafe was the first instant coffee.

A typical eyebrow contains about 550 hairs.

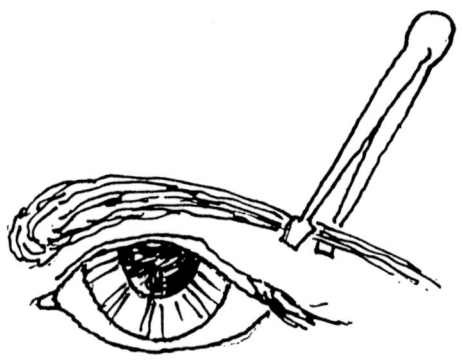

Charles Waite was the first, first-baseman to use this piece of baseball equipment. If you're thinking it was spikes your wrong. It was a glove.

We all know what the word murder means but did you also know that "a murder" is what you call a row of crows.

The liver is the largest organ in the human body.

We have all seen at least one episode of MASH. Do you know what MASH stands for? Mobile Army Surgical Hospital.

On average, there are 2 credit cards for every person in the United States.

We all know what Wilber and Orville Wright were famous for but do you know what other distinction Orville Wright had? He was the pilot in the first fatal plane crash.

The World Trade center in New York City has 208 elevators and 43,600 windows. That means if you were the window washer for that building and you worked five days a week you would have to wash 167 windows a day to finish the building in a year. Good luck.

According to the *Guinness Book of Records,* the heaviest turkey ever raised weighed 86 pounds!

St. Augustine, Florida is the oldest city in the United States but not too many people know that St. Marys, Georgia is the second oldest.

Orson Welles is buried in an olive orchard on a ranch owned by his friend, matador Antonio Ordonez in Sevilla, Spain.

Pittsburgh is the only city where all major sports teams have the same color: Black and gold.

The easiest zip code to remember is 12345 and it is assigned to General Electric in Schenectady, New York.

Panophobia is the fear of everything.

Here are some interesting Acronyms.

~ ~ ~ ~ ~ ~ ~ ~ ~ ~ ~ ~ ~ ~

AM/FM	Amplitude Modulation/Frequency Modulation
BMW	Bavarian Motor Works
URL	Uniform Resource Locator
RAM	Random Access Memory
ZIP	Zone Improvement Plan
Radar	RAdio Detection And Ranging
M&M	Mars & Murray
STP	Scientifically Treated Petroleum
TNT	TriNitroToluene
WD-40	Water Displacement, formula 40
EPCOT	Experimental Prototype Community Of Tomorrow
4-H	Head, Heart, Hands, and Health

In 1920 Ray Chapman a shortstop for the Cleveland Indians, became the only player killed as a result of a major league baseball game. He was hit in the temple with a pitch and died the next day.

In every deck of cards the King of Hearts is sticking his sword through his head. That's why he is often called the "Suicide King".

The Frisbee was originally called the Pluto Platter, but Melin and Kneer changed the name after seeing New England college students throwing pie tins. As they tossed the discs, the students would shout "Frisbee," taken from the Frisbee Baking Co. in Bridgeport, Conn..

When George Washington was elected President, there was a king in France, a czarina in Russia, an emperor in China, and a shogun in Japan. Only the office of President remains today.

Everyone is familiar with the RCA logo Nipper the dog listening to the RCA grammaphone, but the original picture had both the dog and the grammaphone sitting on his dead masters casket. The idea being that the closest thing to his dead masters voice was the RCA grammaphone. The ad was considered to morbid, so they removed the casket.

The ostrich yolk is the largest single cell in the world.

The first zoo in the United States was located in Philadelphia.

Footprints are used by breeders and trainers to identify dogs. Right or Wrong.
Wrong, to identify dogs they use nose prints.

The pea is the oldest known vegetable.

Have you ever wondered what the real name of some movie stars are?

Stage Name	*Real Name*
Mel Brooks	Melvin Kaminsky
Brigitte Bardot	Camille Javal
John Denver	Henry Deutchendorf
Bo Derek	Catheen Collins
Jane Seymour	Joyce Frankenberg
Martin Sheen	Ramon Estevez
Stevie Wonder	Steveland Hardaway

Movie stars who used their real name are:

Marlon Brando	Clint Eastwood
Ursula Andress	Dolly Parton
Clark Gable	Errol Flynn
Dustin Hoffman	Elvis Presley

If your wondering when someone will show up at your door with a check from the Readers Digest contest or one of the other contest, here are your chances of that happening.

◇ ◇ ◇ ◇

Readers Digest --- 1 in 84 million
Publishers Clearing House --- 1 in 182 million
American Family Publishers --- 1 in 200 million
(Good Luck, your going to need it!)

I have always heard that George Washington's teeth were made out of wood. This is not true oh avid book reader. They were made out of whale bone.

Harvard uses "Yale" locks on their buildings.

Contrary to popular belief, cuckoo clocks do not come from Switzerland but from the Black Forest in Germany.

A typical Mayfly lives only one day.

For those of you who thought they knew everything about the Beatles, did you know that they were once known as The Quarrymen?

During a Fall trip to England, Ed Sullivan found himself surrounded by thousands of screaming girls at London's Heathrow Airport. After discovering that four young rock 'n rollers returning from the continent were causing all the fuss, Sullivan signed them to the show without ever hearing them play a note! America was introduced to the Beatles on The Ed Sullivan Show on February 9th. 1964. 73 million people watched the fab four sing "I Want To Hold Your Hand" and "She Loves You." Hundreds of police were called in to handle the mob scene outside the CBS studio 50. By 9 pm that night The Beatles had taken America by storm.

Your hearing is the least sharp of any of the five senses after you have eaten too much.

March 21st. is the first day of the astrological year.

Fun Facts About Beer:

In English pubs, ale is ordered by pints and quarts. So in old England, when customers got unruly, the bartender would yell at them to mind their own pints and quarts and settle down. This is where we get the phrase "mind your P's and Q's".

Many years ago in England, pub frequenters had a whistle baked into the rim or handle of their ceramic mugs. When they needed a refill, they used the whistle to get some service. "Wet your whistle", is the phrase inspired by this practice.

Before thermometers were invented, brewers would dip a thumb or finger into the mix to find the right temperature for adding the yeast. Too cold, and the yeast wouldn't grow. Too hot, and the yeast would die. This thumb in the beer is where we get the phrase "rule of thumb".

The jawbone is the hardest bone in the human body.

Japan is the worlds largest exporter of frog legs.

The tongue weighs practically nothing, but so few people can hold it.

Soccer ledgend Pele's real name was, Edson Aarantes do Nascimento.

Yellowstone National Park built in 1872, was the first national park built but the first area to be set aside under federal protection was Hot Springs National Park in Arkansas in 1832.

The Hoover Dam was built to last 2,000 years. The concrete in it will not fully cure for another 500 years.

Believe it or not, hail is most prevalent in the summer months.

The New York Titans professional football team adopted a new name in 1963. If you guessed the New York Jets, you are right.

Who's army were canned foods developed to feed? You'll be guessing all day so I might as well tell you, Napoleon's Army.

The harmonica in its earliest form was invented by F. Buschmann in 1821. The grandfather of the modern version was invented by Matthias Honer in the 1930's. It was brought to America by German immigrants.

When you see a court document the "V" in the name of a court case does not stand for 'versus', but for 'and' (in civil proceedings) or 'against' (in criminal proceedings).

Have you ever heard the old saying "blood is thicker than water"? Actually, it is six times thicker.

Mexican free-tailed bats sometimes fly up to two miles high to feed or to catch tail-winds that carry them over long distance.

You have probably heard a lot of different explanations of why covered bridges were covered. The real reason for covering timbered bridges was to protect the main timber trusses from the detrimental effects of rain and snow. The intermitant wetting and drying provided an ideal atmosphere for accelerated timber deterioration. Large timber truss bridges were initially built in the United States without covers. It was not uncommon for such a bridge to fail within 10 or 15 years. There are some original covered bridges still standing that have been in place since the 1820's.

Ostriches are the largest living birds. They also are the only birds that have only two toes on each foot.

A group of kittens is called a kindle.

The *"Richelieu"* was one of the heaviest wooden ships ever built. It weighed an unbelievable 9,548 tons and was launched in Toulon, France on December 3, 1873.

The eyes of a snake are covered by clear scales instead of movable eyelids. As a result, their eyes are always open.

Deer have no fixed dens, nesting sites, or homes. They spend their lives wandering an area called a "home range" looking for food.

A pineapple is not like other fruits in one way. A pineapple has to be picked fresh because it will not ripen after it is picked.

Miss Hungary of 1936 had her title taken away because she was underage. It didn't prevent her however from becoming famous. Her name was Zsa Zsa Gabor.

Hair grows at a rate of approximately one hundredth of an inch per day.

Tweety, the cartoon character used to be a baby bird without feathers until the censors made the character have feathers because he "looked naked."

Thank Ed Peterson for your Egg McMuffin. He's the inventor.

Did you ever wonder what's in those crazy "Lava Lamps" created by Craven Walker? Wax and water.

If you live in, work in, or just visit the city a lot Mr. C.C. Magee has cost you money. In 1935, he invented the parking meter.

The song, The Twist was the only 'single' to go to the top of the charts twice. Once in 1959 and again in 1961.

Lou Gehrig was the first major league baseball player to have his number retired.

What are the only two places a dog has sweat glands? I know your on the edge of your seat on this one so I won't keep you in suspense any longer their nose and their paws.

Picture a checker board. You know, black sqaures and red squares. How many squares are there 32, 64, or 72? If you said the middle number, king yourself.

Baseball was the first sport pictured on the cover of Sports Illustrated.

Lightning strikes the Empire State Building more than 50 times a year.

Learn from the mistakes of others. You can't live long enough to make them all yourself.

The cells that make up the antlers of a moose are the fastest growing animal cells in nature.

An ostrich's eye is bigger than its brain.

Did you know that:
A group of cows are a herd.
A group of gorillas are a shrewd.
A group of lions are prides.
A group of seals are rookeries.
A group of fish are a school.

Facts about the Denver International Airport:

~ The total area of the Denver International Airport is 53 square miles, twice the size of Manhattan Island.

~ 2.5 million cubic yards of concrete were used to construct five runways, taxiways and aprons.

~ The fueling system at Denver International Airport is capable of pumping 1,000 gallons of jet fuel per minute through a 28 mile network of pipes.

~ The windows in the control tower are made of distortion-free glass panels and each panel weighs 11,000 pounds.

There is a chemical called "scrooge" which is specially designed to smell bad, much like a skunk's smell but worse. A typical use of "scrooge" is to spray it on doorways of warehouses and unguarded inner city buildings to keep vagrants away.

Christmas is wierd. What other time of the year can you sit in front of a dead tree and eat candy out of socks.

Sears Roebuck and Company operated the first mail order prescription house at the turn of the century. They treated alcoholism with the "White Secret Cure," a mixture that contained opium. They cured the "opium habit" with a cordial that was 40 proof! The new fangled FDA just had no sense of humor about such things unfortunately, so the mail order drug department at Sears was phased out by 1907.

The skin from sharks was once used commercially as sandpaper.

John Wayne turned down the lead in Gunsmoke for fear of being stereotyped as a cowboy.

Vida Blue was the only pitcher to start for both an American League team and a National League team in baseballs all-star game.

Theodore Roosevelt wrote 37 books.

The playing pieces in dominoes are called "bones".

The Vatican is the largest one-person residence in the world.

Over a billion Fig Newton cookies are consumed each year. This makes them the third most popular cookie in America.

Of all the ice cream eaten in the United States, 66% is eaten by adults.

It takes 300 pounds of water to grow one pound of rice.

Some of the finest hardwood in the world grows in Ohio. In fact, one walnut tree in Pioneer Ohio sold for $35,000 in 1975.

You may be suprised to know what part of the human body is most commonly bitten by insects. What do you think? Foot, hand, ear, face? If you said the first one, foot you get the prize.

According to the National Geographic Society, the Nile river is the longest river in the world.

Charles Alderton, a Texas pharmacist, created a soft drink and named it after his prospective father-in-law, Dr. Charles Kenneth Pepper. The doctor was unimpressed, so Alderton dropped the period after the abbreviation for doctor and made his fortune with "Dr Pepper."

He who loses money, loses much;
He who loses a friend, loses more;
he who loses faith, loses all.

Ty Cobb was the first player elected to the Baseball Hall of Fame.

Which do you think is better for our environment, paper or Styrofoam cups? I know you said paper and your wrong. It takes 24 times more power to produce a paper cup. Furthermore, when a paper cup decomposes in a moist landfill it produces methane gas, a threat to add to the greenhouse effect.

In a typical home, there are eight clocks. Take a count and see if your typical.

If you like knives, have knives, or for that matter even know what one looks like, you had better sit down for this fact. The largest "Swiss army knife" was made in England and had 1,973 different blades.

Rhubarb and asparagus are the only two perenial vegetables grown.

The most popular magazine in America is the TV Guide.

Sometimes it is good to practice a favorite skill or hobby just in case you need it someday in real life. Lang Martin of North Carolina can balance seven golf balls, one on top of another. I'm not sure when this is going to come in handy, but I for one am sleeping better knowing he's ready.

I'll bet you don't know what aelurophobia is? It is the fear of cats. How about amaxophobia? It is the fear of riding in a car. I have this one when I ride with my daughter.

Don't try to beat this record.
13 Minutes, 42 seconds is the record for the longest anyone has been known to stay underwater without a breathing apparatus.

The Andy Griffth Show was the first spin-off in TV history. It was a spin-off from the Danny Thomas Show.

There are 20 mathches in a standard pack.

The Library of Congress building, which was built in 1897 contains 327 miles of bookshelves.

The most popular cocktail in the United States is the Martini.

Contrary to a popular misconception, bats are not blind, they do not become entangled in human hair, and they seldom transmit diseases to other animals or humans.

In 1951 it only cost one cent to mail a postcard in the United States.

There are more billionaires living in Texas than in any other state.

In case you didn't know, the Seven Dwarfs did have jobs. They were miners.

The largest number of words put on a single postage stamp is 746, from the country of Greece in the year 1954.

If your alarm clock is not loud enough to wake you up, put it on a tin pie plate. That'll do it.

My hats off to you if you know who this man was. Mr. Kenesaw Mountain Landis. The only clue is "think baseball". For those of you who haven't got it yet, he was the first commissioner of baseball.

Here's a tip to help save your thumb. When you are having difficulty hammering small nails, you can use an ordinary comb to hold the nails while you start them.

Saccharin is 550 times sweeter than cane sugar.

Many Japanese golfers carry "hole in one" insurance, because it is traditional in Japan to buy gifts for all your friends if you have a hole in one.

Vanilla ice cream makes up about 20% of all ice cream sales in the United States.

According to some scientists in England, 70% of the dust in your house is discarded skin cells.

Suppose you play on a amateur baseball team and your opponent doesn't show for the game. They forfeit and you win but what score goes into the record book? If you were thinking 1 to 0 your wrong. It's 9 to 0.

Harvard is the oldest college in the United States.

Mardi Gras Fun Facts

* More than 500,000 king cakes are sold each year in New Orleans between January 6 and Fat Tuesday, and another 50,000 are shipped out of state via overnight courier.

* An economic impact study released by the University of New Orleans estimates that Mardi Gras generates over 500 million annually.

* The largest of about one dozen Mardi Gras supply houses in New Orleans sold 41 million pair of beads for the Carnival in 1991.

* The metro areas 25,000 plus hotel rooms are traditionally 95% filled during Mardi Gras weekend.

Kool-Aid was originally named Kool-Ade, until bureaucrats in the Food and Drug Administration banned the use of the word "ade" because it means "a drink made from..." So inventor E. E. Perkins simply changed the spelling to "aid" meaning "help."

The first night baseball game occurred on May 24, 1935 in Cincinnati.

James Vernor, a pharmacist from Detroit, returned from duty in the Civil War to discover his medicinal ginger tonic had aged quite nicely in his oak barrels. Upon tasting it he realized that it had a much smoother taste than the ginger tonic he had left. He continued to age every batch and that was the birth of Vernor's ginger ale.

When light hits your eye a protein called rhodopsin starts a chemical chain reaction that lets you see. This occurrence is the fastest chemical reaction known.

When people talk about great philanthropists I think they should include the owners of the Cracker Jacks Company. After all they have given away over fifteen billion prizes.

Thirty percent of women color their hair.

Bananas do not grow on trees, they grow on big herb plants.

To handle yourself, use your head.
To handle others, use your heart.

If something like this is really important to you, you can tell a girl crab from a boy crab by their stomachs. A girl crab has a beehive design on its stomach and a boy has a lighthouse.

South Africa used to have two official languages. Now it has eleven.

The first product to have a UPC bar code on its packaging was Wrigley's gum.

Will Clark hit a home run his first time at bat in college, the Olympics, and the Major Leagues.

In Italy, it is illegal to make coffins out of anything except nutshells or wood.

Slightly over 55% of United States households grind their own coffee.

Only six times in history have Time, Newsweek, and Sports Illustrated had the same entity on the cover in the same week. They are Joe Namath, Reggie Jackson, Secretariet, the 1980 U.S. Ice Hockey Team, Mary Lou Retton and O.J. Simpson.

The "you are here" arrow on maps is called an ideo locator. Do you suppose that "ideo" is Spanish for idiot.

Mickey Mouse's ears are always turned to the front, no matter what direction his head is pointing.

Giraffes have no vocal chords.

All elephants walk on tip-toe, because the back portion of their foot is made up of all fat and no bone.

Once a week you should eat something really good, because the lifespan of a tastebud is only ten days. Well, you don't want it to go to the big tounge in the sky never knowing what a good meal tasted like, do you.

Ernie Banks played his entire baseball career for the Chicago Cubs.

The snapping turtle eats carion and for that reason is sometimes used by police to find dead bodies in lakes, ponds and swamps.

A nanominute is one-billionth of a minute.

Yesterday is history,
tomorrow is a mystery,
and today is a gift:
That's why we call it
"The Present".

If you come out of your house tomorrow and see a camel that has only one hump, you will either be looking at an African camel. Or you may have had to much to drink the night before.

George Washington was deathly afraid of being buried alive. He left orders, that after he died, he wanted to be layed out for three days just to make sure he was really dead.

If you are on a ship an see an iceberg you will only be seeing the one-ninth that is above water. In other words, the part of the iceberg that is under water is eight times the size of what you are seeing.

A little math "fun fact".

$$111,111,111$$
$$\times\ 111,111,111$$
$$=\ 12,345,678,987,654,321$$

Bookkeeper and bookkeeping are the only words in the English language with three consecutive double letters.

The first electric Christmas lights were created by a telephone company PBX installer. Back in the old days, candles were used to decorate Christmas trees. This was obviously very dangerous. Telephone employees are trained to be safety conscious. This installer took the lights from an old switchboard connected them together strung them on a tree and hooked them to a battery. I can only wonder if he ever made any money off of this idea, or if was he just the brains behind someone elses millions.

Rabbits love licorice.

Don't use time or words carelessly.
Neither can be retrieved.

The microware was invented after a researcher
walked by a radar tube and a chocolate bar melted
in his pocket.

There are over 1,500 volcanoes in the world.

When opossums are playing "possum" they are
not playing. They actually pass out from shear
terror.

Two thirds of the world's eggplants are grown
in New Jersey.

When the University of Nebraska Cornhuskers
play football at home, the stadium becomes the
state's third largest city.

The reason that firehouses started being built with circular stairways comes from when the engines were pulled by horses. The horses were stabled on the ground floor and they figured out how to walk up straight stairscases.

The only real person to be a "Pez head" was Betsy Ross.

Winston Churchill was born in a ladies room during a dance.

All of the U.S. Presidents have worn glasses, some of them just don't like to be seen with them on in public.

Pinocchio is Italian for "pine head".

Rubber bands last longer when refrigerated.

Frank Sinatra paid a $240,000 ransom to free his kidnaped son.

Presidential First:
> William Howard Taft was the first president to own a car.
> Franklin D. Roosevelt was the first president to have a presidential aircraft.
> Gerald Ford was the first president to have two women try to assassinate him. Both attempts were in California in September of 1975.
> Warren G. Harding was the first president to visit Canada.

What do you think the J&B stands for on a bottle of J&B scotch? Jim and Bob would be to easy. It stands for Justerini & Brooks.

A pig is the only animal that can get sunburned.

Solitaire is the most widely-played card game in the world.

The very first Super Bowl was won by the Green Bay Packers.

Don't give up when you still have something to give. Nothing is really over until the moment you stop trying.

Willie Shoemaker was the first jockey to ride more than 7,000 winners.

Audie Murphy was the most decorated United States soilder of World War II.

The Great Dane is the official dog of the state of Pennsilvania. Pennsilvania is also the only state that has an official Dog.

If a person is a funambulist, does that mean they drive a fun ambulance. No, a funambulist is a tightrope walker.

It doesn't sound like a lot today, but Babe Ruth earned $70,000 in 1927.

Although the name is not used much today, I can still remember my father saying "hand me the monkey wrench". I know if I would have asked how it got its name he would have went into some long story about how a group of monkeys at the St. Louis Zoo got together and invented it. But actually the monkey wrench was invented by Charles Moncke and given the name "Moncke wrench". I guess the name change came with Evolution.

What glass-cleaning device did Mary Anderson invent in 1902? I'll give you a hint. It wasn't Windex, and it was use on automobiles. I think the little light just went off in your head, it was the windshield wiper.

What do you suppose Lawrence Welk had on license plate of his car? Well, A1ANA2 of course.

When I surveyed over one million people and asked them "which is heavier", a baseball or a softball" 70% of them said a baseball. They were right. Actually, I only surveyed 10 people around the office but didn't one million sound more impressive.

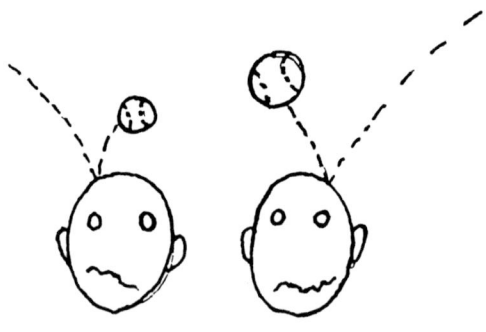

Statistically speaking, what is the safest age of life?   a. 5   b. 10
                        c. 14   d. 27
                        e. 40   f. 52
If you said b, you are correct! If you are reading this now, and you <u>are ten,</u> don't think that this means you can go out and climb the tree your mother said to stay out of.

The Academy Award statue is named after a librarian's uncle. One day Margaret Herrick, librarian for the Academy of Motion Picture Arts and Sciences, made a remark that the statue looked like her Uncle Oscar, and the name stuck.

Elvis Presley had two nicknames for his daughter, Lisa Marie Presley: "Yisa" and "Buttonhead".

The little hard candy, heart shaped mints, with the dumb sayings on them like "kiss me" or "hi sweety" are called Conversation Hearts. They were originally called Motto Hearts when they were created in 1866. During the first six weeks of the year, leading up to Valentines Day on February 14th. over 8 billion of these hearts are sold.

Dave Thomas, the founder of Wendy's, named his business after his daughter, Wendy. The funny thing is that his daughter's name is Melinda Lou. Wendy must have been her nickname.

Barnum's Animal Crackers were introduced in 1902 just before Christmas. Intended to be marketed as a holiday item, National Biscuit Company designed a box that looked just like a circus wagon cage with a string attached so consumers could hang the product from the Christmas tree. Much to their surprise, the product was so popular that Barnum's Animal Crackers became a year round favorite. Over 40 million packages are sold each year. Not bad for something designed to be a Christmas novelty item.

Some people put a lot of thought when choosing a name. Actor Keanu Reeve's first name means "coolbreeze over the mountains" in the Hawaiian language.

The USA is plagued by the most tornadoes.

Princeton and Rutgers were the first two schools to meet for a football game.

A relief pitcher coming into a baseball game gets eight warmup pitches on the playing field.

The first TV Dinner consisted of turkey, sweet potatoes, and peas.

Senior citizens are the biggest carriers of aids. Rollaids - Bandaids - walking aids - medicaid hearing aids - and government aid.

The Triple Crown-winning horse Secretariet, took the 1973 Belmont Stakes by a record setting 31 lenghts.

The first TV commercial went on the air on July 1, 1945 and was sponsored by the Bulova watch company.

Copper makes up ten percent of yellow gold.

Are you old enough to remember these TV Shows and the year in which they first appeared?

Howdy Doody	1947
Your Show of Shows	1950
I Love Lucy	1951
The Mickey Mouse Club	1955
Amos 'n' Andy	1951
Ozzie & Harriet	1952
Davy Crockett	1954
Father Knows Best	1954
Captain Kangaroo	1955

Chia Pets are only sold in December.

If you dislike snakes, don't go to Brazoria County in southeast Texas. This is the only county in the United States and Canada to have every kind of poisonous snake known to these two countries.

I hope you have had as much enjoyment from reading the Fun Facts as I have had from researching and writing about them.

For more information on this book
or one of our other books,
please contact us at:

Evad Enterprises
Po Box 463
O'Fallon, MO 63366

~ ~ ~ ~ ~ ~ ~

The F Book
Fun, Facts, Figures and other F Words

The G Book
Golf facts, jokes, rarities, stories, etc.

The C Book
Tips and reccipes on all types of outdoor
cooking. From camping to barbeques.

~ ~ ~ ~ ~ ~ ~

Coming soon

The S Book
Facts, stories, and rarities on a variety of sports.